From Novice to Pro: Google Pixel Watch User's Handbook

Frank Davis

About This Guide

This guide serves as your indispensable companion in mastering the Google Pixel Watch Series 1 & 2, designed to take you from a novice to a proficient user. Whether you're unboxing your new device or seeking to unlock its full potential, this handbook offers clear and concise instructions, making your journey seamless and enjoyable.

In this book, you'll gain insight into what to expect within its pages, including detailed instructions, tips, and troubleshooting advice. We understand that not all users start with the same level of knowledge, so we ensure that both beginners and those with prior smartwatch experience will find value in these pages.

As you embark on this user-friendly exploration, you'll uncover the wealth of features and functions that the Google Pixel Watch has to offer, from setting up your device to mastering advanced applications. This guide empowers you to harness the full potential of your wearable tech, ultimately transforming you into a pro user.

Table of content

Chapter 1: Introduction

Welcome to the World of Google Pixel Watches

Welcome to the world of Google Pixel Watches, where cutting-edge technology meets stylish design. These watches are your gateway to a smart and connected lifestyle, offering a seamless blend of fashion and functionality. Whether you're a tech enthusiast or a fashion-conscious individual, the Google Pixel Watch Series 1 & 2 has something to offer everyone.

At the heart of this experience is the innovative operating system that powers the Pixel Watches. It's designed to be intuitive and user-friendly, ensuring that you can easily access the features and information you need. The Google Pixel Watch opens up a world of possibilities right at your wrist.

With the ability to make calls, send messages, track your health and fitness, and control your smart home devices, these watches are more than just timekeepers. They are your personal assistant, fitness coach, and style statement all in one.

As you embark on your journey with the Google Pixel Watch, this handbook will be your trusty companion. It will guide you through the unboxing and setup process, introduce you to the watch's interface, and delve into its essential features and advanced functions. You'll also discover tips and tricks to make the most out of your watch and learn how to care for it to ensure a long and rewarding partnership.

So, strap on your Google Pixel Watch and get ready to explore the endless possibilities it brings to your wrist. Welcome to the future of wearable technology!

Getting Started

Getting started with your Google Pixel Watch is an exciting journey into the world of smart wearables. To kick things off, unbox your watch and marvel at its sleek design. Charge it up to ensure it's ready to assist you throughout the day. Next, pair it with your smartphone to unlock its full potential. This simple process connects your watch to your digital life.

Once paired, you can explore the intuitive interface, navigate through watch faces, and access essential features like notifications and fitness tracking. The "Getting Started" phase is your foundation for a seamless and productive experience with your Google Pixel Watch.

What's New in Series 2

Series 2 of the Google Pixel Watch brings a host of exciting enhancements and features, making it a compelling choice for both new users and those upgrading from Series 1. Here's a glimpse of what's new:

1. **Upgraded Performance**: Series 2 boasts a faster processor and improved RAM, ensuring smoother and more responsive performance. Apps load quicker, and interactions are more seamless.

2. **Enhanced Battery Life**: Thanks to optimizations and a more power-efficient chipset, Series 2 delivers extended battery life, allowing you to use your watch for longer between charges.

3. **Additional Health Sensors**: This series introduces new health sensors, including a body temperature sensor and improved heart rate monitoring, enhancing its capabilities as a fitness and health tracker.

4. **Built-in GPS**: Series 2 incorporates built-in GPS, reducing the reliance on a connected

smartphone for accurate location tracking during workouts or outdoor activities.

5. **Advanced Water Resistance**: With improved water resistance, Series 2 can accompany you in more water-related activities, such as swimming, with greater confidence.

6. **Updated Watch Faces**: A fresh collection of watch faces, including customizable options, lets you personalize your watch's appearance to suit your style and mood.

7. **Advanced Voice Recognition**: Google Assistant is even more responsive and capable, enabling you to perform tasks and get information using voice commands.

These enhancements make Series 2 a worthy upgrade, offering a more powerful and versatile smartwatch experience. Whether you're a tech enthusiast or fitness fanatic, the Google Pixel Watch Series 2 has something to offer.

Chapter 2: Unboxing and Setup

Unboxing Your Google Pixel Watch

Unboxing your Google Pixel Watch is the initial step in embarking on an exciting journey into the world of smart wearables. As you gently remove the lid of the box, you're greeted with the exquisite design and craftsmanship of the watch itself. The sleek, modern aesthetics immediately catch your eye, making it a fashion statement as much as a tech gadget.

Beneath the watch, you'll find a carefully arranged assortment of accessories. This typically includes the charging cable, a user manual, and perhaps some additional bands or accessories, depending on the package you've chosen.

Before strapping it on, it's essential to power up your Pixel Watch. Use the included charging cable to connect your watch to a power source. This process is simple and ensures that your watch is ready to assist you throughout the day.

Charging Your Watch

Charging your Google Pixel Watch is a straightforward process that ensures your smartwatch remains operational throughout your busy day. With the included charging cable, connect one end to your watch and the other to a power source, such as a USB adapter or your computer.

The magnetic attachment ensures a secure and effortless connection. While charging, you'll typically see a charging indicator on your watch's screen. The speed of charging may vary, but the process is generally efficient, thanks to the watch's optimized power management.

Pairing with Your Smartphone

Pairing your Google Pixel Watch with your smartphone is a pivotal step in unleashing the full potential of this smart wearable. This seamless connection opens up a world of possibilities, from receiving notifications on your wrist to controlling various aspects of your phone. Here's how to do it:

1. **Activate Bluetooth**: Ensure that Bluetooth is turned on both on your watch and smartphone. This is the fundamental requirement for pairing.

2. **Open the Wear OS App**: On your smartphone, open the Wear OS app, which serves as the bridge between your devices. If it's not already installed, download it from your app store.

3. **Start Pairing**: In the Wear OS app, select "Set up a new watch". Your phone will then search for nearby devices, including your Google Pixel Watch.

4. **Select Your Watch**: When your watch appears on the list, tap to select it. You may see a pairing code on your watch and phone; confirm that they match.

5. **Finalize Pairing**: Follow the on-screen instructions to complete the pairing process. You may be prompted to sign in with your Google account and configure settings.

Once paired, your Google Pixel Watch becomes an extension of your smartphone. You can receive notifications, make calls, control music, and even locate your phone if it's misplaced. This connection seamlessly integrates your digital life into a convenient, wrist-worn package, making your daily activities more manageable and efficient.

Basic Configuration

Basic configuration of your Google Pixel Watch is a fundamental step to tailor your smartwatch to your preferences and needs. Here's a guide on how to get started with the essential settings:

1. **Language and Region**: Begin by choosing your preferred language and region. This ensures your watch's interface is in a language you understand and is set to the correct time zone.

2. **Wi-Fi and Cellular**: Connect your watch to Wi-Fi networks and, if applicable, a cellular plan. This enables you to stay connected, receive updates, and use data-dependent features even when your smartphone is out of reach.

3. **Google Account**: Sign in with your Google account to access services like Google Assistant, Google Pay, and synchronize your data seamlessly across devices.

4. **Display and Watch Face**: Customize the display brightness, screen timeout, and choose a watch face that suits your style. You can also customize complications (widgets) on your watch face to display important information at a glance.

5. **Notifications**: Configure notification preferences, deciding which apps can send alerts to your watch. Tailoring this ensures you're only alerted to what matters most.

6. **Security**: Set up a screen lock or PIN to secure your watch. Biometric options like fingerprint or pattern unlock may also be available.

7. **Health and Fitness**: Enter your personal details and fitness goals for more accurate tracking. Sync with health apps to monitor your activity and progress.

8. **Apps and Widgets**: Install and organize apps and widgets that enhance your daily routine, from weather forecasts to fitness tracking apps.

By completing these basic configurations, you're personalizing your Google Pixel Watch to suit your unique preferences and lifestyle. It becomes a seamless part of your daily routine, delivering timely information and enhancing your digital experience.

Chapter 3: Navigation and Interface

The Watch Face

The watch face on your Google Pixel Watch serves as the focal point of interaction and expression. It's not just about telling time; it's a canvas for personalization and utility. Here's why the watch face is so important:

1. **Personalization**: The watch face is your opportunity to express your style and preferences. With a variety of pre-designed faces and the ability to create your own, you can match your watch to your outfit, mood, or occasion.

2. **Information at a Glance**: The watch face is where you can display essential information like time, date, and your health and fitness stats. This

quick glance at your wrist eliminates the need to pull out your smartphone for routine information.

3. **Widgets and Complications**: Many watch faces allow you to add widgets and complications, displaying data from your favorite apps, such as upcoming appointments, weather forecasts, or step count. This customizable feature makes your watch face a functional hub.

4. **Interactivity**: On touchscreen watches, the watch face can be interactive. You can tap or swipe to access apps, start workouts, or perform tasks like checking notifications.

Touchscreen and Gestures

The touchscreen and gestures on your Google Pixel Watch are the primary means of interacting with this smart wearable, making navigation and control intuitive and efficient. Here's how these elements work together:

Touchscreen:

Your watch's touchscreen is the central control panel, allowing you to access apps and features. You can swipe to scroll through notifications, menus, and apps. Tapping on icons or buttons opens apps and initiates actions. It's a familiar and user-friendly interface for anyone accustomed to smartphones.

Gestures:

Gesture controls are designed to enhance the user experience, especially when your hands are busy or when touch isn't convenient. Here are some common gestures:

1. **Wrist Gesture**: By raising your wrist to your face, your watch's display automatically turns on. This gesture ensures you can quickly view notifications without needing to tap the screen.

2. **Quick Access**: When you're in an app or on the watch face, a swipe down from the top of the screen opens the quick settings menu, where you can toggle settings like Wi-Fi, Do Not Disturb, and more.

3. **Notifications**: You can swipe left or right on a notification to dismiss or interact with it. For example, swipe to the left to access actions like reply or mark as read.

4. **App Switching**: Swiping left or right on the watch face allows you to switch between recently used apps, making multitasking a breeze.

Notifications and Quick Settings

Notifications and Quick Settings are pivotal aspects of your Google Pixel Watch's interface, ensuring that you stay connected and in control with ease and efficiency.

Notifications:

1. **Instant Alerts**: Your watch serves as an extension of your smartphone, delivering real-time notifications right to your wrist. These notifications include messages, calls, emails, and alerts from various apps, providing a quick and convenient way to stay informed.

2. **Interactivity**: You can interact with notifications directly on your watch. For instance, responding to messages, dismissing alerts, or accepting or rejecting calls without reaching for your phone.

3. **Customization**: You have control over which apps can send notifications to your watch, allowing you to filter and prioritize information to suit your preferences.

Quick Settings:

1. **Effortless Control**: Quick Settings are your shortcut to essential watch functions. Swipe down from the top of the screen, and you can instantly access features like Wi-Fi, Do Not Disturb, brightness control, and battery saver mode.

2. **Convenience**: Adjusting settings becomes a breeze, and you can quickly toggle on or off various functions to match your immediate needs, whether it's silencing notifications during a meeting or activating Wi-Fi to check messages when your phone is out of range.

Navigating Apps

Navigating apps on your Google Pixel Watch is a seamless and convenient experience, thanks to the smartwatch's user-friendly interface and touchscreen capabilities. Here's how you can efficiently navigate and interact with apps:

App Drawer:

- Start by tapping the center button on your watch face to open the app drawer. This is where you'll find all the apps installed on your watch.
- Swipe vertically to scroll through the apps. You can tap an app to open it.

Recent Apps:

- You can quickly access recently used apps by swiping from left to right on the watch face.
- This "recent apps" menu allows you to switch between apps without returning to the app drawer.

Gestures:

- Some apps support swipe gestures for navigation. For example, you might swipe up or down to scroll through messages or notifications within an app.
- These gestures are designed for a smooth and intuitive experience, making it easy to interact with content.

Voice Commands:

- Google Assistant is integrated, allowing you to open apps and perform actions using voice commands. Simply say, "Hey Google", followed by your request.

Quick Access:

- You can customize your watch face with app shortcuts, allowing you to launch specific apps with a quick tap. This is particularly useful for your most frequently used applications.

Navigating apps on your Google Pixel Watch is intuitive and tailored to the compact, wrist-worn form factor. The touchscreen interface, gesture support, and voice recognition ensure that you can access and interact with your favorite apps with ease, making your watch a versatile companion for both productivity and entertainment.

Chapter 4: Essential Features

Health and Fitness Tracking

Health and fitness tracking is at the core of the Google Pixel Watch experience, promoting an active and healthy lifestyle while providing valuable insights into your well-being. Here's how the watch excels in this area:

Activity Monitoring:
- The watch employs a combination of sensors to track your physical activity accurately. It counts your steps, monitors your heart rate, and calculates the calories you burn, providing a comprehensive overview of your daily movements.

Workout Tracking:

- Whether you're jogging, cycling, swimming, or practicing yoga, the Google Pixel Watch offers tailored workout modes. It records data specific to each activity, such as distance, pace, and heart rate, offering a detailed summary of your exercise.

Heart Rate Monitoring:

- Continuous heart rate monitoring keeps you informed about your heart's performance. It's an invaluable tool for tracking trends in your resting heart rate and detecting potential health issues.

Sleep Tracking:

- The watch also delves into the quality of your sleep, providing insights into your sleep patterns, including sleep duration, interruptions, and the stages of sleep. This data helps you optimize your sleep routine.

Stress Management:

- With stress monitoring, you'll receive feedback and guidance to help manage daily stress levels. This feature enhances your mental well-being by encouraging relaxation techniques and mindfulness.

Nutritional Insights:

- Pair your watch with health apps to keep track of your nutrition. You can log your meals and monitor your caloric intake to maintain a balanced diet.

Fitness Goals:

- Set and track fitness goals through the watch, whether it's a target step count, weight loss, or training for a specific event.

Messaging and Calls

Messaging and calls are essential functions of your Google Pixel Watch, allowing you to stay connected on the go without the need to pull out your smartphone. Here's how the watch excels in these areas:

Messaging:

1. **Notifications**: Your watch seamlessly receives notifications for text messages, emails, and various messaging apps. You can read these messages directly on your watch's screen, making it a quick and discreet way to stay informed.

2. **Quick Replies**: When you receive a message, you can reply with predefined or custom responses. This feature ensures you can acknowledge messages without taking out your phone.

3. **Voice-to-Text:** Google Assistant integration allows you to dictate replies, transforming your spoken words into text messages. It's convenient when you need a more detailed response.

Calls:

1. **Answer and Make Calls**: You can answer incoming calls directly on your watch. The watch includes a speaker and microphone for hands-free communication.

2. **Quick Responses**: If you can't take a call immediately, you can send a quick response or decline the call from your watch.

3. **Call Logs**: Access your call history to see missed, received, and dialed calls.

4. **Built-in Speaker**: The watch's speaker is useful not only for calls but also for listening to music, podcasts, and taking advantage of voice commands.

Music and Media

Music and media capabilities on the Google Pixel Watch offer entertainment and convenience on your wrist. Here's how it enhances your multimedia experience:

Music Control:

1. **Control on the Go:** You can control your phone's music playback directly from your watch. Play, pause, skip tracks, and adjust volume without having to retrieve your smartphone.

2. **Local Storage**: Some smartwatches, like Series 2, may have local storage, allowing you to store music directly on your watch. This means you can enjoy your favorite songs even when your phone isn't nearby.

Media Streaming:

1. **Spotify and Other Apps**: Popular music streaming services like Spotify often have companion apps for smartwatches. You can browse and control your playlists without needing your phone.

Notifications:

1. **Media Alerts**: Your watch receives media notifications, letting you know when a new podcast episode, song, or video is available. You can launch the respective app directly from the notification.

Voice Commands:

1. **Google Assistant**: You can use voice commands to play music or search for songs. For instance, you can say, "Hey Google, play my workout playlist" to initiate your preferred workout tunes.

Health and Fitness Integration:

1. **Music for Workouts**: Your watch can play your favorite workout playlist to keep you motivated during exercise. It syncs with health and fitness apps to enhance your workouts.

The music and media features make your Google Pixel Watch a versatile entertainment companion. Whether you're on a jog, relaxing at home, or in the midst of a workout, your watch ensures you're always a button press or voice command away from your favorite songs and media content. This integration simplifies your digital life, all from the convenience of your wrist.

Google Assistant

Google Assistant is the digital AI companion that significantly enhances the functionality and convenience of your Google Pixel Watch. Here's why it's a standout feature:

Voice Activation:

- By simply saying "Hey Google" or "Okay Google", you wake up Google Assistant, enabling voice commands and searches without touching your watch. This hands-free interaction is especially useful when you're on the go or busy.

Information at Your Fingertips:

- Google Assistant provides answers to questions, delivers weather updates, and offers information on a wide range of topics. Whether you need to check the weather, convert units, or settle a bet with a friend, it's like having a knowledgeable friend on your wrist.

Smart Home Control:

- If you have a smart home, Google Assistant can control compatible devices. Adjust your thermostat, turn off the lights, or check who's at the door with voice commands.

Reminders and Notifications:

- You can set reminders and receive proactive notifications on your watch. Never forget an important task or miss a calendar event.

Navigation and Directions:
- Google Assistant offers turn-by-turn directions, whether you're driving or walking, helping you navigate your way through unfamiliar places.

App Integration:
- It seamlessly integrates with various apps, allowing you to send messages, make reservations, or initiate actions in supported third-party apps.

Voice Typing:
- Google Assistant enables voice typing, making it easy to compose messages or search the web without a physical keyboard.

Customization Options

Google Assistant is the digital AI companion that significantly enhances the functionality and convenience of your Google Pixel Watch. Here's why it's a standout feature:

Voice Activation:

- By simply saying "Hey Google" or "Okay Google", you wake up Google Assistant, enabling voice commands and searches without touching your watch. This hands-free interaction is especially useful when you're on the go or busy.

Information at Your Fingertips:

- Google Assistant provides answers to questions, delivers weather updates, and offers information on a wide range of topics. Whether you need to check the weather, convert units, or settle a bet with a friend, it's like having a knowledgeable friend on your wrist.

Smart Home Control:

- If you have a smart home, Google Assistant can control compatible devices. Adjust your thermostat, turn off the lights, or check who's at the door with voice commands.

Reminders and Notifications:
- You can set reminders and receive proactive notifications on your watch. Never forget an important task or miss a calendar event.

Navigation and Directions:
- Google Assistant offers turn-by-turn directions, whether you're driving or walking, helping you navigate your way through unfamiliar places.

App Integration:
- It seamlessly integrates with various apps, allowing you to send messages, make reservations, or initiate actions in supported third-party apps.

Voice Typing:
- Google Assistant enables voice typing, making it easy to compose messages or search the web without a physical keyboard.

Google Assistant transforms your Google Pixel Watch into a versatile tool for information, productivity, and smart home control. Its responsive and adaptable nature simplifies tasks and enhances your daily routines, making your watch more than just a timepiece – it's a proactive and intelligent companion on your wrist.

Chapter 5: Advanced Functions

App Installation and Management

App installation and management on your Google Pixel Watch are vital for enhancing its functionality. These aspects make your watch a versatile tool tailored to your unique needs.

App Installation:

1. **Wear OS Play Store**: Your watch has access to the Wear OS Play Store, a curated selection of apps designed for wearable devices. You can browse and install apps directly on your watch.

2. **Companion Apps**: Some apps on your phone may have companion apps for your watch, enhancing the watch's capabilities. For instance,

fitness apps can sync data, and messaging apps allow for quick responses.

3. **Local Storage**: If your watch, like Series 2, has local storage, you can install apps directly on the watch. This is useful for apps you want to use independently of your phone.

App Management:

1. **App Grid**: Organize your apps in a grid layout for easy access. You can arrange them based on your preference, ensuring your most-used apps are readily available.

2. **Uninstallation**: If an app is no longer useful, you can uninstall it from your watch to free up space and streamline your app list.

3. **Updates**: The watch ensures your apps are up to date by handling app updates automatically, so you always have the latest features and improvements.

Wi-Fi and Cellular Connectivity

Wi-Fi and cellular connectivity are essential features of the Google Pixel Watch, offering flexibility and independence from your smartphone while ensuring you stay connected. Here's how these connectivity options enhance your smartwatch experience:

Wi-Fi Connectivity:

1. **Data Access**: Your watch can connect to available Wi-Fi networks, allowing you to use apps and access data even when your phone is out of Bluetooth range. This is particularly useful if you want to leave your phone behind but remain connected.

2. **Firmware Updates**: Wi-Fi connectivity ensures that your watch's firmware is always up to date. It's an efficient way to receive the latest features and security patches.

Cellular Connectivity:

1. **Stand-Alone Operation**: If your Google Pixel Watch supports cellular connectivity, you can make and receive calls, send messages, and use data without relying on your smartphone. This independence is especially handy during workouts or when you prefer to travel light.

2. **Emergency Calls**: Cellular connectivity provides peace of mind by allowing you to make emergency calls even without your phone nearby. This feature can be a lifesaver in critical situations.

3. **Streaming and App Use**: Cellular-enabled watches let you stream music, access apps, and use navigation services directly on your watch. You're not limited by the range of your phone's connection.

4. **Data Synchronization**: Cellular connections ensure that your watch is always in sync with your

digital life, including email, calendar events, and messaging apps.

Smart Home Control

Smart home control is a powerful and convenient feature of the Google Pixel Watch, allowing you to manage your connected devices directly from your wrist. Here's how it enhances your home automation experience:

Device Compatibility:

1. **Wide Range of Devices**: The watch typically works with a broad range of smart home devices, such as lights, thermostats, doorbells, cameras, and more. It's compatible with popular platforms like Google Home and others.

Voice Commands:

1. **Google Assistant Integration**: Google Assistant, accessible on your watch, serves as a hub

for voice-controlled commands. You can adjust the thermostat, turn on lights, lock doors, or perform other actions with simple voice commands, making it convenient and hands-free.

Quick Access:

1. **Quick Settings**: Smart home controls are often accessible through the quick settings menu on your watch. With a few taps, you can adjust the brightness, change the temperature, or control your connected devices.

Notification Alerts:

1. **Alerts and Notifications**: Your watch can alert you to important events or triggers in your smart home, such as motion detection, doorbell rings, or unusual changes in your home environment.

Geofencing:

1. **Location-Based Automation**: Use your watch's geofencing capabilities to set up automation

rules based on your location. For instance, you can have your lights turn on when you arrive home.

Smart home control on your Google Pixel Watch turns your wrist into a remote control for your entire home. It adds convenience, security, and a touch of futuristic living to your daily routine, making your watch more than a timepiece; it's a powerful home automation hub.

Battery Optimization

Battery optimization is a crucial aspect of the Google Pixel Watch experience. To ensure your watch lasts through the day and beyond, it offers several strategies for conserving power:

1. **Battery Saver Mode**: When the battery runs low, you can activate Battery Saver Mode to extend your watch's uptime. This mode reduces

background activity and notifications, ensuring essential functions remain operational.

2. **Screen Brightness**: Adjust the screen brightness to an appropriate level to save power. Lower brightness settings reduce energy consumption.

3. **Screen Timeout**: Configure the screen timeout to ensure the display turns off quickly when not in use, preserving battery life.

4. **App Management**: Keep an eye on apps consuming excessive power and consider uninstalling or limiting their usage.

5. **Background App Restrictions**: Restrict background app activity to prevent unnecessary power drainage.

Battery optimization helps your Google Pixel Watch remain functional and reliable throughout the day, so you can enjoy its features without the worry of running out of power.

Troubleshooting

Troubleshooting common issues with your Google Pixel Watch is essential to ensure it functions seamlessly. Here are some tips to address potential problems:

1. **Charging Issues:**
- If your watch doesn't charge, ensure the charger and watch contacts are clean and properly aligned. Try a different power source or cable to rule out charging problems.

2. **Connectivity Problems:**
- If your watch doesn't connect to your phone, make sure Bluetooth is enabled on both devices. Restart both your watch and phone, and ensure they're in close proximity.

3. **Battery Drain**:

- Excessive battery drain might be due to background apps or settings. Check which apps are consuming power and consider disabling unnecessary features like Wi-Fi, location, or always-on display.

4. **App Crashes**:

- If apps are crashing, uninstall and reinstall them from the Wear OS Play Store to fix potential software glitches.

5. **Screen Unresponsiveness**:

- If your screen isn't responding, try restarting your watch. If it persists, perform a factory reset as a last resort.

6. **Software Updates:**

- Regularly check for software updates, as they often include bug fixes and improvements.

7. **Notifications**:
- If you're not receiving notifications, verify that you've configured notification settings correctly for your preferred apps.

8. **Fitness and Health Tracking**:
- Inaccurate fitness or health data might be due to incorrect sensor placement. Ensure the watch is snug on your wrist and positioned correctly.

Troubleshooting these issues can help you keep your Google Pixel Watch running smoothly. If problems persist, consulting the user manual or contacting customer support may be necessary.

Chapter 6: Tips and Tricks

Battery Saving Tips

To extend your Google Pixel Watch's battery life, consider these essential battery-saving tips:

1. **Screen Brightness**: Lower the screen brightness to a level that's still comfortable to read but not overly bright.

2. **Screen Timeout**: Set a shorter screen timeout, so the display turns off quickly when not in use.

3. **Battery Saver Mode**: Activate Battery Saver Mode when the battery is running low to reduce background activity.

4. **Background Apps**: Limit or restrict background app activity to prevent unnecessary power consumption.

5. **Wireless Functions**: Disable Wi-Fi and cellular connectivity when not needed, and turn off location services.

6. **App Management**: Keep an eye on power-hungry apps and consider uninstalling or reducing their usage.

These tips help you maximize your watch's battery life, ensuring it remains functional throughout the day.

Personalization and Watch Faces

Personalization and watch faces are at the heart of the Google Pixel Watch experience, allowing you to make your smartwatch truly your own. The watch faces serve as both a style statement and an information hub. Here's why they matter:

1. **Style Expression**: With a plethora of watch faces to choose from, you can select one that

complements your fashion sense, mood, or occasion. You can go from classic to playful, minimalistic to data-rich.

2. **Information at a Glance**: Watch faces serve as a quick reference point for vital information like time, date, weather, and health stats. Customizable complications provide even more data at your fingertips.

3. **Variety**: The wide selection of watch faces ensures that you can change your watch's appearance frequently to match your outfit or your daily activities.

4. **Interactive Features**: Some watch faces allow for interactivity, letting you tap or swipe to access apps, initiate actions, or customize the appearance.

Hidden Features

Exploring the Google Pixel Watch reveals some intriguing hidden features that can enhance your overall experience:

1. **Auto-Unlock**: If you use a paired Android phone, your watch can automatically unlock your phone when it's nearby, making the transition between devices seamless.

2. **Find My Phone**: In the event your phone goes missing, you can use your watch to locate it, even if it's on silent, by making it ring.

3. **Emergency SOS:** Hidden within the power menu is an Emergency SOS feature that allows you to quickly call for help or share your location with trusted contacts in case of an emergency.

4. **Customizable Buttons**: On some models, you can customize the physical buttons to perform

specific actions, making navigation and app access more convenient.

5. **Multiple Time Zones**: If you frequently travel, your watch can display multiple time zones simultaneously, ensuring you're always aware of the time back home and at your current location.

6. **Translation Tools:** Your watch can assist with translations, letting you speak into it, and it will translate your words into another language.

These hidden features showcase the versatility and practicality of your Google Pixel Watch, making it more than just a timepiece—it's a companion with various unexplored capabilities that can simplify your daily life.

Productivity Hacks

Productivity hacks can maximize your Google Pixel Watch's utility in your daily life. Here are some tips to make your watch a productivity powerhouse:

1. **Voice Commands**: Utilize Google Assistant for quick tasks like setting reminders, creating to-do lists, or sending messages without the need to type.

2. **Quick Settings Customization**: Personalize your quick settings menu to include the most-used functions, such as Do Not Disturb or screen brightness, for swift access to essential controls.

3. **App Notifications:** Customize which apps send notifications to your watch, ensuring you're alerted only to the most important updates.

4. **Voice Typing**: For longer messages or emails, use voice typing instead of typing on the watch's small keyboard.

5. **Calendar and Email**: Sync your calendar and email apps to receive alerts for important appointments and messages right on your wrist.

6. **Fitness and Health Tracking**: Leverage the watch's health and fitness features to monitor your activity, set fitness goals, and enhance your well-being.

By optimizing your Google Pixel Watch for productivity, you can save time, stay organized, and manage your daily tasks more efficiently, making the watch a valuable tool for both work and personal life.

Updates and Future Features

Updates and future features play a pivotal role in the continued evolution of the Google Pixel Watch, ensuring it remains cutting-edge and adaptable to users' needs. Here's why they are essential:

Regular Updates:

1. **Bug Fixes**: Updates often include bug fixes and performance enhancements, ensuring your watch runs smoothly and reliably.

2. **Security Patches**: Timely updates address security vulnerabilities, keeping your personal data and device safe from threats.

3. **New Features**: Updates frequently introduce new features and improvements, expanding the watch's capabilities and offering an enhanced user experience.

Future Features:

1. **Enhanced Health Tracking**: Future updates may bring advanced health monitoring features, such as ECG capabilities or stress detection, enhancing its role as a wellness device.

2. **Deeper Integration**: Expect closer integration with smart home devices and broader compatibility with third-party apps, making the watch a more versatile hub.

3. **Customization**: Future features may include additional watch faces and customization options to tailor the watch to individual preferences.

As technology advances, the Google Pixel Watch's firmware updates and future features promise to keep it at the forefront of smartwatch innovation, offering even more value and utility to users. Whether it's for health and fitness, communication, or personalization, these updates ensure your watch stays relevant and useful.

Chapter 7: Maintenance and Care

Cleaning and Maintenance

Proper cleaning and maintenance are essential for keeping your Google Pixel Watch in top condition, ensuring its longevity and functionality. Here are some guidelines for maintaining your watch:

Cleaning:

1. **Regular Wiping:** Clean the watch's screen and body regularly using a microfiber cloth. This prevents dust, sweat, or dirt buildup that can affect the touch screen and sensors.

2. **Water Resistance**: If your watch is water-resistant, rinse it under clean water after exposure to saltwater or chlorine, then wipe it dry. Avoid using soap or hot water.

3. **Band Care**: For removable bands, clean them separately by following the manufacturer's care instructions.

Maintenance:

1. **Software Updates**: Keep your watch's software up to date to ensure it runs smoothly and securely.

2. **Charging**: Use the provided charger and avoid overcharging your watch. Charging to 80% can prolong the battery's life.

3. **Storage**: When not in use, store your watch in a cool, dry place, away from extreme temperatures or direct sunlight.

4. **Strap Replacement**: If your watch has a replaceable strap, consider changing it regularly to keep your watch looking fresh and avoid discomfort from worn-out bands.

5. **Protection**: Consider using a screen protector or protective case to safeguard against scratches and minor impacts.

Proper cleaning and maintenance habits can extend the life of your Google Pixel Watch and ensure that it continues to serve you effectively. Regular care not only preserves the watch's appearance but also maintains its performance and functionality.

Warranty and Support

Warranty and support services are essential aspects of owning a Google Pixel Watch, providing peace of mind and assistance when issues arise. Here's why these services are crucial:

Warranty:

1. **Coverage**: The warranty typically covers manufacturing defects and malfunctions for a

specified period, offering free repairs or replacements within this duration.

2. **Quality Assurance**: A warranty underscores the manufacturer's confidence in the product's quality and reliability.

3. **Financial Protection**: It protects your investment, ensuring you don't have to bear the cost of repairs for covered issues.

4. **Consumer Rights**: A warranty is often legally required in many regions, protecting consumers' rights and ensuring they receive functional products.

Support:

1. **Technical Assistance**: Support services provide technical help for setup, troubleshooting, and general inquiries, making it easier to resolve common issues.

2. **Software Updates**: Manufacturers offer support by providing software updates to address bugs and improve functionality.

3. **Repairs**: In the case of hardware issues or out-of-warranty problems, support services can guide you on where to get your watch repaired or serviced.

4. **Knowledge Sharing**: Support often includes resources like user manuals, forums, and online guides for maximizing your watch's potential.

Warranty and support services offer valuable safeguards and resources for Google Pixel Watch users, ensuring their investment is protected and that they have access to assistance when needed.

Safety Guidelines

Safety guidelines are important for ensuring the safe and responsible use of your Google Pixel Watch. Here are some key safety measures to consider:

1. **Water Resistance**: If your watch is water-resistant, understand its specific rating and limitations. Don't submerge it in water deeper than recommended, and always dry it thoroughly if it gets wet.

2. **Cleaning**: Use a microfiber cloth to clean your watch. Avoid abrasive materials that can scratch the screen or body. If the watch comes into contact with liquids or chemicals, clean it immediately.

3. **Charging**: Use only the provided charger and follow the manufacturer's guidelines for charging. Avoid overcharging, which can impact battery health.

4. **Temperature**: Extreme temperatures can affect your watch. Avoid exposing it to excessive heat, direct sunlight, or prolonged cold, as these can harm the battery and display.

5. **Allergies**: If you have sensitive skin or allergies, consider using hypoallergenic bands or covers, especially if you experience skin irritation.

6. **Updates**: Keep your watch's software up to date to ensure it functions correctly and securely.

7. **Repairs**: Avoid attempting to repair the watch yourself. If you encounter issues, consult the manufacturer's support or warranty services.

8. **Emergency Calls**: In case of an emergency, familiarize yourself with how to make calls or use the emergency SOS feature on your watch.

By following these safety guidelines, you can ensure the responsible and secure use of your Google Pixel Watch, keeping yourself and your device in good health and condition.

Chapter 8: Conclusion

Summary

In summary, the Google Pixel Watch offers a multifaceted and versatile smartwatch experience. From health tracking to productivity, messaging, and smart home control, it's a dynamic companion for modern living. The ability to personalize watch faces, coupled with hidden features and regular updates, ensures it remains relevant and adaptable to individual needs. With an emphasis on battery optimization and safety guidelines, users can maintain their watches effectively while maximizing their potential. Furthermore, warranty and support services provide assurance and assistance. As technology evolves, the Google Pixel Watch's commitment to updates and future features promises to keep it at the forefront of smartwatch innovation, ensuring it remains a valuable part of the wearer's daily life.

Final Thoughts

In conclusion, the Google Pixel Watch is more than just a timekeeping device; it's a versatile and dynamic companion that caters to various aspects of modern life. Its extensive features, from health and fitness tracking to messaging and smart home control, position it as a valuable tool for productivity, convenience, and entertainment. Personalization options and watch faces allow users to express their individual style while providing quick access to essential information.

The watch's commitment to regular updates and future features ensures that it remains at the forefront of smartwatch innovation, adapting to changing needs and technologies. Battery optimization and safety guidelines underscore the watch's durability and responsible use.

Moreover, the inclusion of warranty and support services offers peace of mind to users, knowing they have assistance in case of issues. The Google Pixel Watch is not just a gadget; it's a holistic solution for staying connected, managing your health, and enhancing your daily routines. As it continues to evolve, it promises to be an indispensable part of modern living.

Resources and References

For additional resources and references regarding the Google Pixel Watch, consider the following:

1. **Official Website**: Visit the official Google Pixel Watch website for in-depth product information, updates, and support.

2. **User Manuals**: The user manual that comes with your watch provides valuable insights into its features, setup, and troubleshooting.

3. **Online Communities**: Participate in online forums and communities where users discuss tips, tricks, and solutions for common issues with the Google Pixel Watch.

4. **Tech Blogs:** Technology blogs and websites often provide reviews, tutorials, and news related to the latest features and updates for smartwatches.

5. **Manufacturer Support**: Contact the manufacturer's support for technical assistance, warranty queries, and other inquiries related to your watch.

These resources and references can help you make the most of your Google Pixel Watch and keep it functioning at its best.

www.ingramcontent.com/pod-product-compliance
Lightning Source LLC
Chambersburg PA
CBHW071306050326
40690CB00011B/2550